THE SECRETS OF THE WORLD WIDE WEB

Discover the new trends and tools of the World Wide Web, and use them to both raise awareness, membership, and money and foster innovation in business processes such as product development, marketing, sales, and support.

Jescy Karl

The Secrets of the World Wide Web

ISBN 978-0-9816421-2-3

Verticalbit.com
Design . Publish . Promote

USA - UK - CAN

Dedication

To God, my family, parents, and friends !

"Do your part to live in peace with everyone, as much as possible"
Romans 12:18

TABLE OF CONTENTS

INTRODUCTION

CHAPTER 1 - THE WORLD WIDE WEB

CHAPTER 2 - THE NEW WEB OR WEB 2.0

CHAPTER 3 - NEW WEB, NEW TOOLS

CHAPTER 4 - NEW TOOLS, NEW STRATEGIES

INTRODUCTION

The secrets of the World Wide Web is a quick guide to business process innovation using the latest web trends and tools. This book focuses on how to use the web to create results in the value chain of an organization. It is an excellent source of information for users that wish to catch up with the latest web technologies. This edition offers a close glance at topics such as:

- The World Wide Web
- The New Web or Web 2.0
- New Web, New Tools
- New Tools, New Strategies

You will discover chapters and sections on how to use the web to raise awareness, membership, and money. You will also learn how to apply the web to foster innovation in business processes such as product development, marketing, sales, and support.

How to Use This Book

This book begins with the nuts and bolts, and progresses through the subject in a way that can build your knowledge. At the end of each chapter, you will find a list of examples and online resources for additional details. The book is painless to read, and contains no technical lingo.

Chapter 1, The World Wide Web, defines the World Wide Web, Hypertext, HTML (Hypertext Markup Language), and HTTP (Hypertext Transfer Protocol). You will also learn about web standards, web content, and users.

Chapter 2, The New Web or Web 2.0, describes the patterns of the new web. It covers topics such as the web as a platform, harnessing collective intelligence, and design patterns.

Chapter 3, New Web, New Tools, reviews the most recent tools on the web such as wikis, blogs, social networks, and social interaction tools.

Chapter 4, New Tools, New Strategies, demonstrates how to use web technologies and trends to generate values in the value chain of an organization.

How This Book Is Organized

Each chapter of this book starts with a short introduction followed by goals, sections, and online resources.

The goals of the chapter list the objectives you will reach after reading the chapter.

The sections contain text, figures, and tables serving to explain the concepts of the chapter.

The online resources section provides a list of websites that you can visit to get further details on the concepts of the chapter.

Reader Services

We take every measure to ensure the accuracy of our content. However, if you find any error in the book, please report it at verticalbit.com. Also you can subscribe to receive the latest updates, and downloads for this book.

Online Resource

- **Publisher's website** - www.verticalbit.com

CHAPTER 1 - THE WORLD WIDE WEB

In 1989, Tim Berners-Lee proposed to CERN (European Organization for Nuclear Research) an information system that would permit physicists around the world to collaborate, and share information. He then implemented the system and called it the World Wide Web. Today this system has become the primary channel for important conversations such as politics, education, healthcare, businesses, jobs, family, entertainment, and more. So what is the World Wide Web?

At the completion of this chapter, you will be able to:

- Define the World Wide Web
- Describe Web technologies
- Understand Web content
- Identify Web users
- Describe Web Tools
- Explain the 2001 dot-com crash

What is the World Wide Web?

The World Wide Web, generally called the Web, is a service of the Internet. Tim Berners-Lee implemented the Web using four technologies: Markup language, Hypertext, the Internet, and Client/Server computing. He wrote the first web client and server in 1990. His specifications of URI (Uniform Resource Identifier), HTTP (Hyper-Text Transfer Protocol), and HTML (HyperText Markup Language) were refined later by W3C (World Wide Web Consortium).

Markup Language

Markup is a set of annotations to text that give instructions on how it is to be displayed. Markup languages have been available in computer typesetting and word-processing systems years before 1989. Tim Berners-Lee used them to invent HTML for the web.

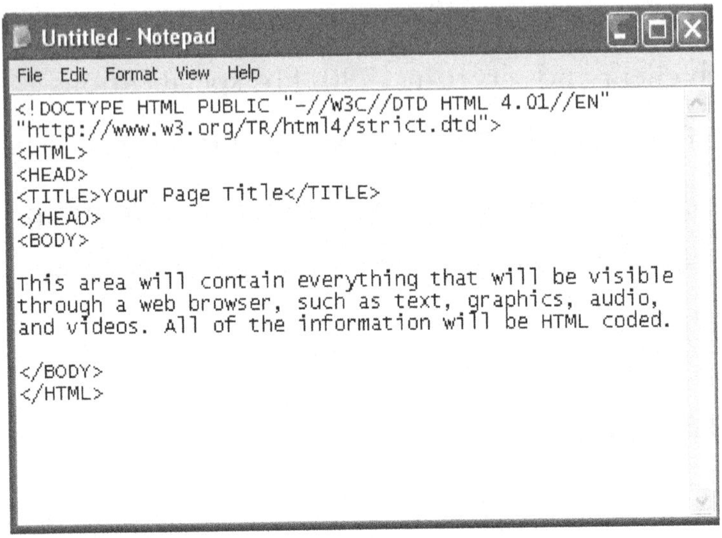


```
<!DOCTYPE HTML PUBLIC "-//W3C//DTD HTML 4.01//EN"
"http://www.w3.org/TR/html4/strict.dtd">
<HTML>
<HEAD>
<TITLE>Your Page Title</TITLE>
</HEAD>
<BODY>

This area will contain everything that will be visible
through a web browser, such as text, graphics, audio,
and videos. All of the information will be HTML coded.

</BODY>
</HTML>
```

A simple HTML page

Hypertext

Hypertext is a way for embedding links to documents, pictures, audios, videos, programs and other elements in text. It makes possible a dynamic organization of information through links and connections, called hyperlinks.

The Internet

The Internet and the Web are often used interchangeably but they aren't the same thing. The Internet is a network of computer networks allowing users to access services such as email, telnet, web, and more.

The history of the Internet began with ARPANET, a project of the US Department of Defense to create a fault-tolerant computer network that would continue to function even in the event of a nuclear or natural disaster.
The first stage of the Internet included ARPANET and attached mainframe computers on dedicated connections.

The second phase involved adding desktop PCs which connected through telephone wires. The third stage added wireless connections to laptop computers. Today the Internet includes servers, personal computers, laptops, and mobile devices. It allows connectivity from literally everywhere on earth, and in outer space using dial-up, wireless, satellite, and broadband connections.

Client/Server Computing

The World Wide started as a collection of hypertext documents, called web pages, linked to one another via the Internet like a spider web. These documents are stored on computers called web servers located around the world. Using a web browser (client), one can search, and view these web pages.

Client/Server Computing

Tim Berners-Lee created the first web server, web browser (client), and the Hypertext Transfer Protocol (HTTP). In

December 1990 he implemented the first successful communication between an HTTP client and server via the Internet.

In computer network engineering, a request for comments (RFC) is a memorandum published by the Internet Engineering Task Force (IETF) describing methods, behaviors, research, or innovations applicable to the working of the Internet and Internet-connected systems. HTTP is described in RFC 2616. It is an application-level protocol. The http client (web browser) and server use the reliable TCP/IP (Transmission Control Protocol/Internet Protocol) protocol to establish a connection.

Each machine connected to the Internet has an address known as an IP (Internet Protocol) address. The IP address takes the form of four numbers separated by dots (e.g. 10.3.5.10). To make it easy to remember, the Internet use a distributed Internet database known as DNS (Domain Name System) to convert IP addresses to text names called domain names. For example 10.3.5.10 can be translated to yourcompany.com.

Every domain name ends in a top-level domain name, which is the group of letters following the final dot - .com,. net, .org, .biz, .tv, .mobi, .gov, .us, .uk, .ca, etc. ICANN (Internet Corporation for Assigned Names and Numbers) operates the Internet Assigned Numbers Authority (IANA) and is in charge of maintaining the DNS for the top-level domain names. ICANN delegates the management of most top-level domains to responsible organizations called registrars.

To use a domain name like yourcompany.com, you will need to register it with a registrar. To publish a web page for yourcompany.com, you will need to store the HTML file of the web page on a web server, usually referred as web host.

Viewing the content of a web page on the web normally begins either by typing the address (URL) of the page into a web browser, or by following a hyperlink to that page. The web browser then initiates a series of communication messages behind the scenes, in order to fetch and display the page.

First, the server-name portion of the URL is resolved into an IP address using the top-level DNS servers. This IP address is necessary to contact and send data packets to the web server. The browser then requests the resource by sending an HTTP request to the web server at that particular address. In the case of a typical web page, the HTML text of the page is requested first and parsed immediately by the web browser, which will then make additional requests for images and any other files that form a part of the page. Having received the required files from the web server, the browser then renders the page onto the screen as specified by its HTML, and style sheets. Any images and other resources are incorporated to produce the on-screen web page that the user sees.

Standards and Specifications

By the end of 1992, several web browsers appeared. The most notable of these was Mosaic, developed at NCSA. By mid-1995, there were two major browsers, Microsoft Internet Explorer, and Netscape. Development was rapid and both Microsoft and Netscape were adding new features continuously.

At the same time W3C, headed by Tim Berners-Lee, released many standards and technical specifications to define the operation of different aspects of the World Wide Web. Here are a few:

- **Recommendations for markup languages**, especially HTML and XHTM. These define the structure and interpretation of hypertext documents.

- **Recommendations for style sheets**, especially CSS (Cascading Style Sheets).

- **Recommendations for JavaScript** and DOM (Document Object Model).

Also IETF (Internet Engineering Task Force) released additional publications that provide definitions of other essential technologies for the World Wide Web, including, but not limited to:

- **URI (Uniform Resource Identifier)**, which is a universal system for referencing resources on the Internet, such as hypertext documents and images. URIs are often called URLs (Uniform Resource Locators).

- **HTTP (Hypertext Transfer Protocol)**, as defined by RFC 2616: http://1.1 and RFC 2617: HTTP Authentication, which specify how the browser and server authenticate each other.

- **RTP (Real-time Transport Protocol)**, which defines a standardized packet format for delivering audio and video over the Internet. It was developed by the Audio-Video Transport Working Group of the IETF and first published in 1996 as RFC 1889, and superseded by RFC 3550 in 2003. RTP is frequently used in streaming media systems (together with the RTSP - Real Time Streaming Protocol) as well as in videoconferencing and push to talk systems. For these, RTP carries media streams controlled by H.323

or Session Initiation Protocol (SIP) signaling protocols. RTP is the technical foundation of the Voice over IP industry.

Web users

At the beginning, the web was used primarily by academic institutions, scientists and the government for research and communications. However in 1992, the nature of the web changed suddenly by the U.S. government's decision to pulling out of the internet management, and let commercial entities offer Internet access to the general public.

"The web is more a social creation than a technical one. I designed it for a social effect — to help people work together — and not as a technical toy. The ultimate goal of the Web is to support and improve our web-like existence in the world. We clump into families, associations, and companies. We develop trust across the miles and distrust around the corner."
- Tim Berners-Lee

In 1995, the World Wide Web gradually began receiving a great deal of attention in the popular culture, and the mass media. By 1996, companies started using the web not only to advertise but also to sell products and services.

Web Tools

The period 1995-2000 saw the emergence of many sites, and tools. These one way, read-only tools helped users and companies get the most out of the web. For examples, we had:

- **Double-Click:** a company, founded in 1996 that develops and provides Internet ad serving services.
- **Ofoto**, an online photography service, was started in June 1999. Ofoto started by simply allowing users to upload JPEG images to the online service, share online photo albums with friends, and purchase prints of photos.
- **Mp3.com**, founded in November 1997, provided information about digital music, artists, and songs. It was named after the popular music file format, MP3.

- **Britannica Online:** is a general English-language encyclopedia.
- **Personal websites:** World Wide Web pages created by an individual to contain content of a personal nature.
- **Domain name speculation:** The domain name speculation refers to buying domains with the intent of selling them later for a higher price. The main target of domain name speculation is generic words which can be valuable for the dominant position they would have in any field due to their descriptive nature.

Web directories: A web directory or link directory is a directory on the World Wide Web. A web directory is not a search engine and does not display lists of web pages based on keywords; instead, it lists web sites by category and subcategory.

The 2001 Dot-com Bubble

The period 1995-2000 has seen the creation of a vast Internet-based companies commonly referred to as dot-coms. A combination of fast increasing stock prices and individual speculation in stocks produced thousands of millionaires. Many of these businesses dismissed standard business models, and focused on increasing market share at the expense of the bottom line. As a matter of fact, the dot-coms ended up to a bubble, and crashed in 2001.

After the dot-com crash of 2001, business and technology strategists expressed the need for new ideas. In October 2004, O'Reilly and MediaLive organized a conference on the matter and came up for the first time with the term of Web 2.0. What is web 2.0? This is the subject of the next chapter.

Online Resources

- **TCP/IP suite** - http://en.wikipedia.org/wiki/Internet_protocol_suite
- **European Organization for Nuclear Research** (CERN) - http://public.web.cern.ch/public/
- **The Internet** - http://en.wikipedia.org/wiki/Internet
- **The World Wide Web Consortium** (W3C) - http://www.w3.org/

CHAPTER 2 - THE NEW WEB OR WEB 2.0

The term web 2.0 describes the changing trends in the use of the web following the aftermath of the 2001 dot-com crash. At the completion of this chapter you will be able to:

- Define web 2.0
- Describe web 2.0 rules
- Understand web 2.0 patterns
- Predict the future of the Web

What is Web 2.0?

Tim O'Reilly defines web 2.0 in the following terms:

"Web 2.0 is the network as platform, spanning all connected devices; Web 2.0 applications are those that make the most of the intrinsic advantages of that platform: delivering software as a continually-updated service that gets better the more people use it, consuming and remixing data from multiple sources, including individual users, while providing their own data and services in a form that allows remixing by others, creating network effects through an "architecture of participation," and going beyond the page metaphor of Web 1.0 to deliver rich user experiences."
- Tim O'Reilly

Tim Berners-Lee describes it this way:

"Web 1.0 was all about connecting people. It was an interactive space, and I think Web 2.0 is of course a piece of jargon, nobody even knows what it means. If Web 2.0 for you is blogs and wikis, then that is people to people. But that was what the Web was supposed to be all along."
- Tim Berners-Lee

The concept of web 2.0 came about during a conference brainstorming session lead by Tim O'Reilly. The objective was to show that the web did not collapse but instead got to a turning point in 2001. The brainstorming session showed clear new trends in the way the Web is being used.

WEB 1.0	**VS**	**WEB 2.0**
DoubleClick	-->	Google AdSense
Ofoto	-->	Flickr
Akamai	-->	BitTorrent
Mp3.com	-->	Napster
Britannica Online	-->	Wikipedia
Personal websites	-->	Blogging
Domain speculation	-->	Search engine optimization
Page views	-->	Cost per click
Screen scraping	-->	Web services
Publishing	-->	Participation
CMSs	-->	Wikis
Directories (taxonomy)	-->	Tagging ("folksonomy")
Stickiness	-->	Syndication

Brainstorming Session of Web 2.0 Vs Web 1.0

The Rules of Web 2.0

Tim O'Reilly and MediaLive also came out with obvious philosophical, social, and technical differences. For example, they identified "participation", as the main rule of Web 2.0. They also recognized the following key elements: The Web as a Platform, Harnessing Collective Knowledge, and Rich User Experience.

The Web as a Platform

The idea behind this concept is the web has become a platform to get things done, besides of a place to read information. Presently the web is in use for:

Cloud computing: Cloud computing is described as internet-based distributed computing. This can be hardware, software, and service. For example cloud computing software is real-time software delivered "as a service" over the Internet to users.

Social Interactions: Voice and video conversations, instant messaging, text messaging, social communities, wikis, blogs, webmail, and other social interaction tools.

Entertainment: Music downloads, TV shows, movies, and games.

Harnessing the Collective Intelligence

Web 2.0 focuses a lot on social interactions. It brings the development and evolution of web culture communities. It creates a new environment which includes:

Social networking: Web culture communities such as social-networking sites, video sharing sites where users share talents, and create new relationships. Here are a few examples: myspace.com, facebook.com, linkedin.com, and youtube.com.

Crowd sourcing: New business strategy that facilitates dialogue, participation, collaboration, and sharing. Examples of crowd-sourcing tools are wikis, RSS feeds, blogs, bookmarking, and tagging.

Mahsups: A web application that combines data from more than one source into a single integrated tool. An excellent example of mashup is the Google map which is a mashup of cartographic data, photos, videos, Wikipedia articles, and transit information.

Rich User Experience

The evolving technology infrastructure in computers, wireless, telecommunications, digital medias, Internet technologies, and programming has also brought new design patterns.

Usability and Accessibility: Most modern websites are goal-oriented, easy to use and access. They have the information that users need, and use words, pictures, and colors that make sense to the users.

Desktop-like User Experience: Ajax has prompted the development of interactive websites that mimic desktop applications, such as word processing, spreadsheets, and slideshow presentations. These websites offer features and applications similar to a PC environment, as well as the added ability of being able to run within any modern browser. For example WYSIWYG wiki sites replicate many features of PC authoring applications. Other sites perform collaboration and project management functions.

Multi-device Interfaces: The PC is no longer the only access device for internet applications. These are now built to integrate services across handheld devices, PCs, and internet servers.

The web has become a read-write, participatory web.
The concept of the web as a participation platform and the evolving technology infrastructure of the digital age brought new rules, patterns, and capabilities that go beyond what the public formerly expected in the environment of the so-called "Web 1.0".

What about Semantic Web?

People usually confuse Web 2.0 with Semantic Web (SW). Web 2.0 involves people's participation, collaboration, and interactions. Semantic web is about common formats for integration and combination of data drawn from diverse sources. It provides a common framework that allows data to be shared and reused across applications. It is a collaborative effort led by W3C with participation from a large number of researchers and industrial partners.

The Future of the Web

The future of the web depends on its core components which are: Internet, web technologies, web content, standards, and users. People are already talking about web 3.0 but don't be dupe by those buzzwords. Instead keep track of the evolutions that are happening in the online world to improve people creativity and collaboration, web technologies, and contents. These are fundamental and will shape the future of the World Wide Web. The next chapter will focus on the tools of the new web environment.

Online Resources

- **Web 2.0** - http://en.wikipedia.org/wiki/Web_2.0

- **Dot-com bubble** - http://en.wikipedia.org/wiki/Dot-com_bubble

- **Tim O'Reilly**, 10/1/2005 -http://radar.oreilly.com/archives/2005/10/web_20_compact_definition.html

- **Tim Berners-Lee**, 07/28/2006 - http://www.ibm.com/developerworks/podcast/dwi/cm-int082206.txt
- **Semantic Web (SW)** - http://www.w3.org/2001/sw/

CHAPTER 3 - NEW WEB, NEW TOOLS

People are now living in a connected world. They expect to access information and entertainment anytime and anywhere they happen to be. At the completion of this chapter, you will be able to:

- Describe the digital environment
- Understand the social platform tools
- Describe the social content tools
- Explain the social interactions tools

The digital environment

The users of the digital age are most of the time connected to the Internet using broadband connections or wireless networks. They use different digital devices to upload various type of content to the web. They are also expecting audio, video, picture, and different types of services from their digital devices. They want these to work together to share content. Here is a partial list of consumer digital devices:

- Music players
- Video players
- Digital cameras
- Cell phones
- Smart phones

- Console gaming systems
- Digital video recorders
- PC to TV extenders
- Digital entertainment centers
- Mobile Internet devices
- Portable gaming devices
- Portable navigation systems with embedded cellular chip
- In-car navigation systems with wireless internet link
- Digital photo frames

Social Platform Tools

People of the connected age also use a multitude of social platform tools to collaborate, and socialize on the web.

Social media community

A social media service focuses on building online communities of people who share interests and/or activities. Most social network services are web based and provide a variety of ways for users to interact.

Social medias let people create a profile and then make friends, communicate, find jobs and love, share content, documents, photos, audio files, video clips, and other information. Social networking websites are now being used regularly by millions of people around the world. Examples of social networking tools and services are linkedin.com, myspace.com, and facebook.com.

Wikis

A wiki is a page or collection of web pages designed to enable anyone who accesses it to contribute or modify content, using a simplified markup language.

Wikipedia.org

Wikis are often used to create collaborative websites and to power community websites. The collaborative encyclopedia Wikipedia is one of the best-known wikis. Wikis are used in business to provide intranet and knowledge management systems.

Social Content Tools

The users of the connected age deliver various types of social content to the web. They produce content such as text, photos, audio, and videos. They use different tools to publish and organize content on the web.

Blogs

A blog, a contraction of web log, is an online diary or journal usually maintained by an individual or an organization.

A typical blog combines text, images, and links to web pages, and media related to its topic. Many blogs let readers comment the content in an interactive format. Blogs are primarily text but can also be:

- **Photograph** – photoblog: flikr.com
- **Video** – vlog: YouTube.com
- **Audio** – podcasting

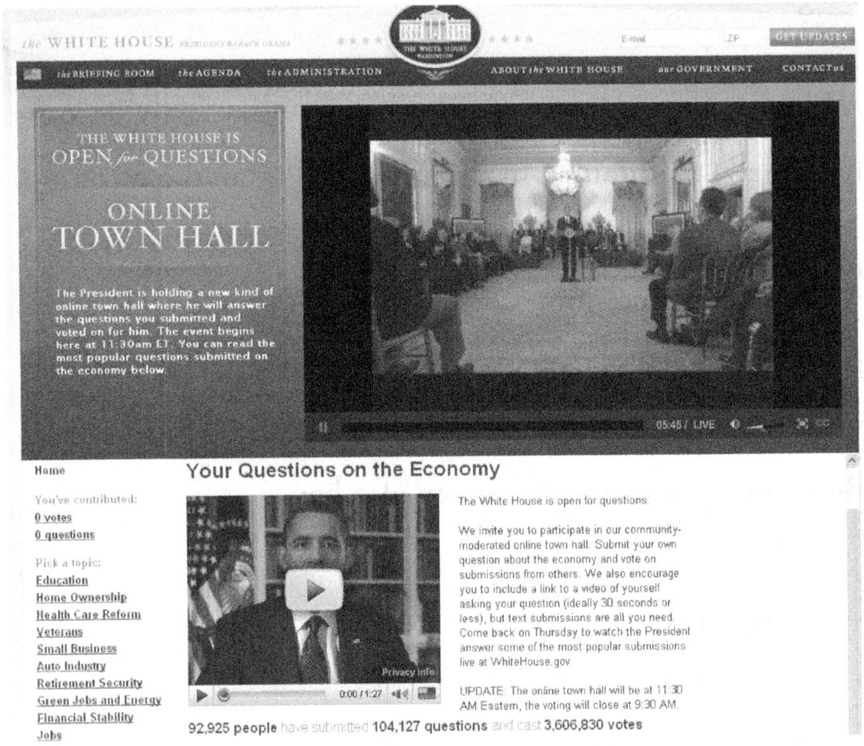

Blog of the Whitehouse.gov

Bookmarks and Tagging

- **Social bookmarking** is a web tool that groups web pages, blog posts, articles, and multimedia files.

- **Tagging** is a web tool that assigns keywords to bookmarked articles, blog posts, photos, podcasts, and videos.

- **Folksonomy** is another web tool that filters and classifies the bookmarked and tagged objects on the web, and makes them searchable. Examples of folksonomies are del.icio.us, digg, and technorati.

Social Interactions Tools

The conversations of the digital age are being held on the web using social interactions tools such as: micro-blogging, webmail, instant messaging, text messaging, video and voice over IP, events and calendars, social media mining, and cloud computing.

Micro-blogging

Micro-blogging is a form of multimedia blogging that allows users to send brief text updates or macromedia such as photos or audio clips and publish them, either to be viewed by anyone or by a restricted group chosen by the user.

These messages can be submitted by a variety of means, including text messaging, instant messaging, email, digital audio or the web.

The content of a micro-blog differs from a traditional blog due in that it is typically more topical, smaller in aggregate file size. People utilize micro-blogging for both business and individual reasons. Many micro-blogs provide a short commentary on a person-to-person level, or share news about a company's products and services.

The most notable micro-blogging service is twitter.com. Other leading social networking websites like facebook.com, myspace.com, and linkedin.com also have their own micro-blogging feature, better known as status updates.

Webmail

Webmail is a web-based e-mail service intended to be primarily accessed via a web browser, as opposed to through an e-mail client, such as Microsoft Outlook, or Mozilla's Thunderbird. Very popular webmail providers include Gmail, Yahoo! Mail, Hotmail and AOL. A major advantage of web-based email over application-based email is that users can access their inboxes from any Internet-connected computer around the world.

Instant messaging

Instant Messaging allows users to send instant messages to each other over the internet. Popular instant messaging tools are Google Talk, Skype, MSN messenger, and AOL.

Text messaging

Short Message Service (SMS) is a communication protocol allowing the interchange of short text messages between mobile telephone devices. Text messaging is the most widely used data application on the planet; most of the mobile phone subscribers can send and receive text messages on their phones. The SMS technology has facilitated the development and growth of text messaging.

Video conferencing and VoIP

Voice and video over IP tools allow users to make telephone and video conferencing calls over the Internet. Skype and Google Talk are two examples.

Events and calendars

Event and calendar tools let users keep track of events, coordinate schedules, stay on schedule, promote and share events and calendars, create invitations, and send reminders. You can set up automatic event reminders, including mobile phone notifications, and instantly bring up anything on your calendar with the built-in search tool.

Social media mining

The users of the digital age keep track of what's happening on the web using search alerts or mining, and feed subscription tools.

Search alerts are email updates of the latest relevant search engines and blogs search results based on a specific query or topic. For example Google Alerts currently offers several types of alert searches such as news, blogs, videos, and groups.

RSS (Really Simple Syndication) is a family of Web feed formats used to publish frequently updated works such as blog entries, and news headlines. RSS formats are specified using XML (Extensible Markup Language), a generic specification for the creation of data formats. These are then broadcasted over RSS. Web feeds benefit publishers by letting them syndicate content automatically. They benefit readers who want to subscribe to timely updates from favored websites or to aggregate feeds from many sites into one place. Users can subscribe to those feeds for a subject of their interests using software called an "RSS reader", "feed reader", or "aggregator", which can be web-based, desktop-based, mobile device or any computerized Internet-connected device. Examples of RSS feed readers are Google reader, Yahoo reader, and most web browsers.

Cloud computing

Cloud computing is Internet-based development and use

of computer technology. It is a business information management style of computing in which typically real-time resources are provided "as a service" over the Internet to users. For example, cloud-based office applications include online editing and sharing of text files, spreadsheets, chats, emails, calendars, and online meeting tools.

Online Resources

- **Google Alerts** - http://www.google.com/alerts
- **Social Media** - http://en.wikipedia.org/wiki/Social_media
- **Cloud Computing** - http://en.wikipedia.org/wiki/Cloud_computing

CHAPTER 4 - NEW TOOLS, NEW STRATEGIES

The digital age has dramatically changed our social and economic behaviors. The consumers' expectations are no more the same. At the end of this chapter you will be able to:

- Describe the new trends in consumers' expectations
- Use Web 2.0 in Product Development
- Apply Web 2.0 in Marketing
- Apply the latest web tools in Sales and Support
- Use Web 2.0 to raise awareness, membership and money.

Trends in consumers' expectations

Today's consumers have become their own broadcasters using text, graphic, audio, video, and print. They use devices that deliver various types of content to the web. They expect content to be downloadable, portable, and accessible anywhere, anytime, and on-demand. They also want content to be sharable, and ready for real-time collaboration.

They rely on the web to work, interact, and get entertainment. They use a multitude of interaction tools such as wikis, blogs, social media sites, IM, webmail, text messaging, VoIP, cloud-computing, and videoconferencing. As a result, the Web has become an extremely dynamic place that is being updated at a breath-taking rate. News sources are adding timely stories; bloggers are posting their ideas online; and users are reviewing products on vendors' web-sites, publishing their latest pictures, podcasts, and videos on the social media services.

This new environment has offered many new opportunities to individuals, companies, and organizations. They are now using the web space to raise awareness, membership, and money. They are also applying the web to foster innovation in business processes such as product development, marketing, sales, and support.

Product Development

The conventional methods in product development are now overturned. While conventional consumer research, based on surveys, provides an essential foundation in product development, it no longer represents a competitive edge. Modern companies are now tapping into consumers' minds, and passions to get upfront ideas, co-develop products, solutions, and growth. Using a community tool, organizations can create systems and processes that let consumers, partners, employees, and investors participate in all the steps of the product development process: Research, Product definitions, Product specifications, Testing, Sales and Support. A good example can be seen at ideastorm.com, the Dell's web community.

Research

Blogs are regular space for sincere conversations. Consumers persistently share their views, experiences, complaints and opinions about products, brands and companies on thousands of blogs, and community sites. Information trapping on blogs, and search engines, can help find out what consumers are saying on a specific product, and identify the trends with the hottest momentum. Taking the time to watch or mine blogs for common themes and insights can provide a plentiful source of fresh, consumer-inspired ideas. A company can monitor for:

- Key employees
- Company name
- Products
- Consumer hangouts
- Competitors
- Blogs and social content
- Social bookmarks and tags
- Industry with strong momentum.

RSS (Really Simple Syndication), and Google Alerts provide an easy way for companies to track what's being discussed on topics of interest.

Product definitions

Employees, partners, and consumers can submit ideas and vote for the best ones. In addition, they can create product or service definitions for those ideas.

Product specifications

Employees and partners can define product or service specifications.

Testing, Sales, and Support

Employees, partners, and consumers can test prototypes, add improvements, and provide supports.

Marketing

The Internet has changed the medium of mass communication and the traditional ways have lost serious grounds with the generations of the digital age. Websites like del.icio.us, flickr.com, facebook.com, myspace.com, linkedin.com, digg.com, youtube.com, and newsvine.com become new channels to reach consumers. These types of sites serve as portals to people everywhere and are delivering media in the form of pictures, blogs, video clips, and feeds. By understanding how these sites work, you can leverage them to reach your market in ways that were not possible before.

Company brochures, press releases, websites, search engine optimization, and banner ads are still in use but now there are more creative ways to get the word out. For example, companies can create buzz marketing to increase product anticipation and target a specific demographic. Video clips, news, and pictures can now be released through social networking sites in order to gain brand equity and increase product awareness. By understanding and taking advantage of these tools, you can be more innovative and find new ways to implement marketing campaigns without relying on heavy advertising budgets.

Companies can use social networking sites to drive traffic to their websites, find consumers with specific interests, and determine company or industry trends with strong momentum. Using a company blog, organizations can also market subtly the company's products, services, and ideas while helping consumers find the best solutions for their needs.

Sales and Support

Marketing and sales are now integrated. Marketing departments combine their traditional marketing processes with social media marketing to attract prospects. Web technologies have armed sales representatives with outstanding new tools to attract, interact, and manage customers and prospects. Web 2.0 tools such as IM, Liveperson, VoIP, and Video conferencing allow sales representatives to provide instant communication to prospects while they are browsing the website. Prospects get their questions answered right away. Sales representatives move the buying process forward using technologies such as online contracts, and payment systems. They also use web-based CRMs (Customer Relationship Management) systems to retain customers' information, track activities, and actions.

After the sale, companies use online communities and social networking to get product feedback, generate grass roots' ideas, provide customer support, and foster collaboration and crowd-sourcing. Many companies let users take over the support process of their products and services.

Raising Awareness, Membership, and Money

Modern organizations are using the web to raise awareness, connect with likely donors, raise funds, find volunteers, and other substantial benefits. They do that by using the new web tools to attract supporters, build relationship, and call for actions.

Attracting supporters

Attracting supporters starts with a usable, interactive, and goal-oriented website. This Allows the organization to communicate its missions, keep the supporters around, and call for actions on its behalf.

- **A usable website** has fresh content with a consistent look-and-feel. It communicates the right message to the target supporters using words, and pictures that make sense to them.
- **An interactive website** empowers supporters with the ability to communicate using interactive features like document sharing, blogs, comments, text and instant messaging, VoIP, and video chats. An interactive website will make

potential supporters feel involved, and most likely will take actions on behalf of the organization.

- **A goal-oriented website** calls for actions from supporters. It makes it easy for them to subscribe, donate, contact and chat with the organization, share comments, and take other actions that achieve the goals of the organization.

Build Relationship

Social medias activities can offer a complete network of users on a website. One way to accomplish this is to provide to individuals possibilities to create memberships, manage personal profiles, make friends, select topics of interest and ways to be contacted (text messages, email, phone, and so on). Inform supporters about the issues that are important to them and the organization.

Calling for actions

Motivate supporters to take actions and rally on behalf of the organization's missions through social medias, email, traditional mail, phone, fax, or even door-to-door. Take advantage of the viral nature of the Internet and let supporters share the organization's story with friends and parents via emails and other social media channels. Give them the ability to make online donations, subscribe to newsletters and RSS feeds, and sign up for volunteers.

The nominee of the democratic party of the 2008 US presidential election, Barack Obama, used web 2.0 tools to raise awareness, membership, and funds. This is a good model that can be used for many organizations to promote ideas, recruit supporters, and raise money. To see what this website looked like during the electoral campaigns, go to archive.org , and search for barackobama.com.

Online Resources

- **Dell uses a forum tool** to let users post ideas for new or improved products. Users also can comment ideas, and vote for the best ones. http://www.ideastorm.com.
- **Cable News Network (CNN)** uses the website ire-port.com to gather news around the world.
- **Also YouTube.com** is another model of product created by using the labor of the crowd.
- **Harvard Business Channel on YouTube.com** - http://www.youtube.com/watch?v=9WX7BNnYTf8&feature=channel_page

ALPHABETICAL INDEX

About the Author

Jescy Karl is an information systems scientist with deep knowledge in Internet technologies, operating systems, databases, and programming. He's been a user of the World Wide Web since 1994.

Made in the USA
Monee, IL
04 November 2026

67378301R00056